Our Baffling Planet

Harold the Raindrop

Books by Marnie

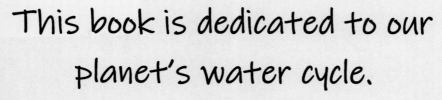

This book is dedicated to our planet's water cycle.
Keep on flowing!

© Marnie Christensen. All Rights Reserved.

No part of this book may be reproduced, stored in a retrieval system, or transmitted by any means without the written permission of the author.

First published February 24, 2024
ISBN: 978-1-7388853-7-4

This is Harold.

Harold is a raindrop.

Raindrops like Harold are made out of
teeny, tiny water droplets.

Lots and lots of them.

They get these water droplets
from the cloud they were born in.

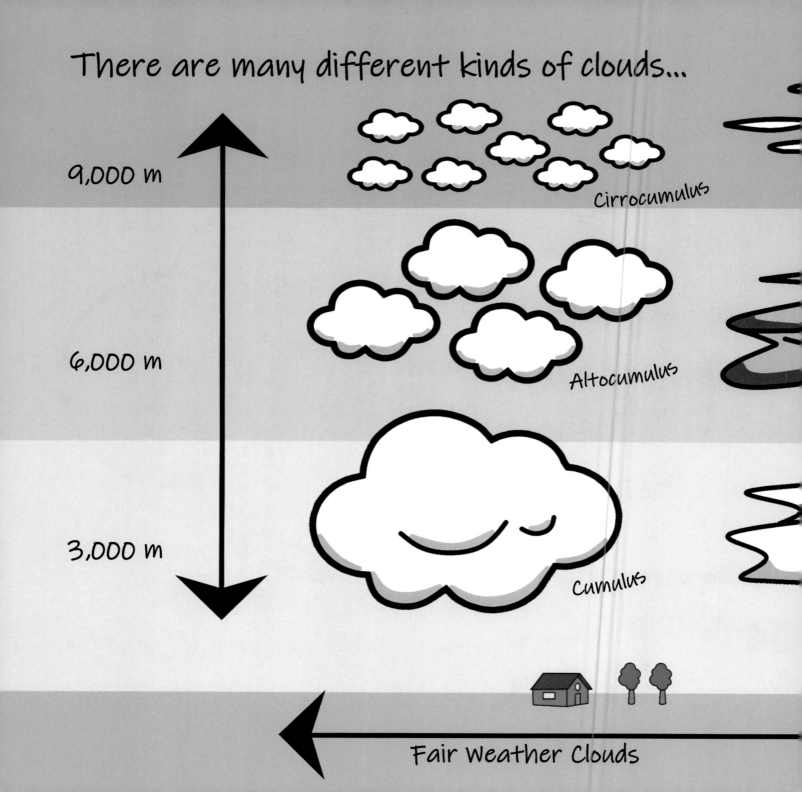

Big clouds up in the sky are made up entirely of water droplets and dust particles, called nuclei.

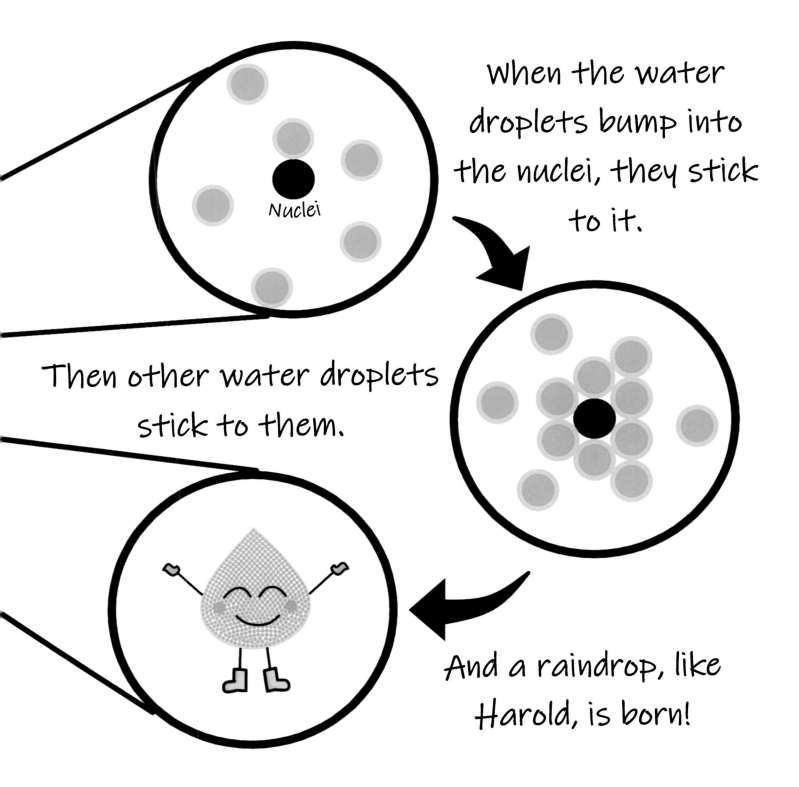

Nuclei

When the water droplets bump into the nuclei, they stick to it.

Then other water droplets stick to them.

And a raindrop, like Harold, is born!

when raindrops have 1 million water droplets, they are heavy enough to fall from the cloud.

This is called **precipitation**.

Harold loves falling from his cloud! He can fall as many different kinds of forms.

Rain   Snow

Sleet   Hail

Like a raindrop, a snowflake forms around a nuclei. But the water droplets are supercooled (below 0°C) and freeze when they touch it.

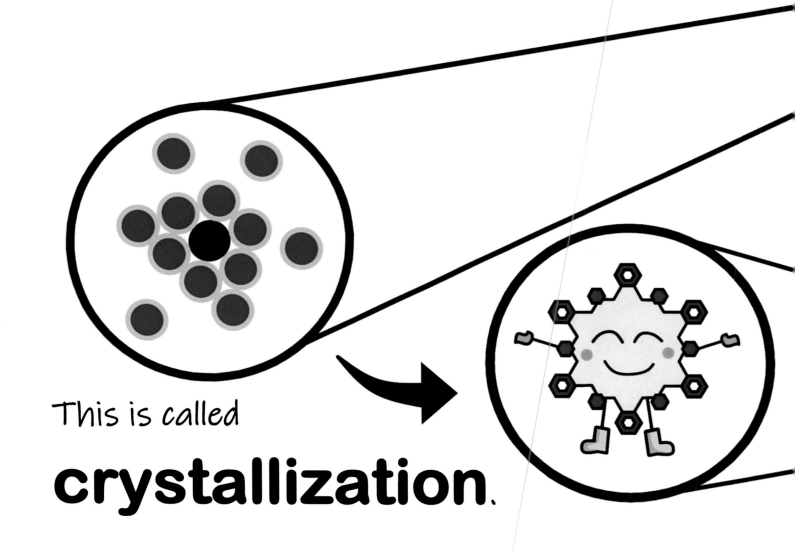

This is called
crystallization.

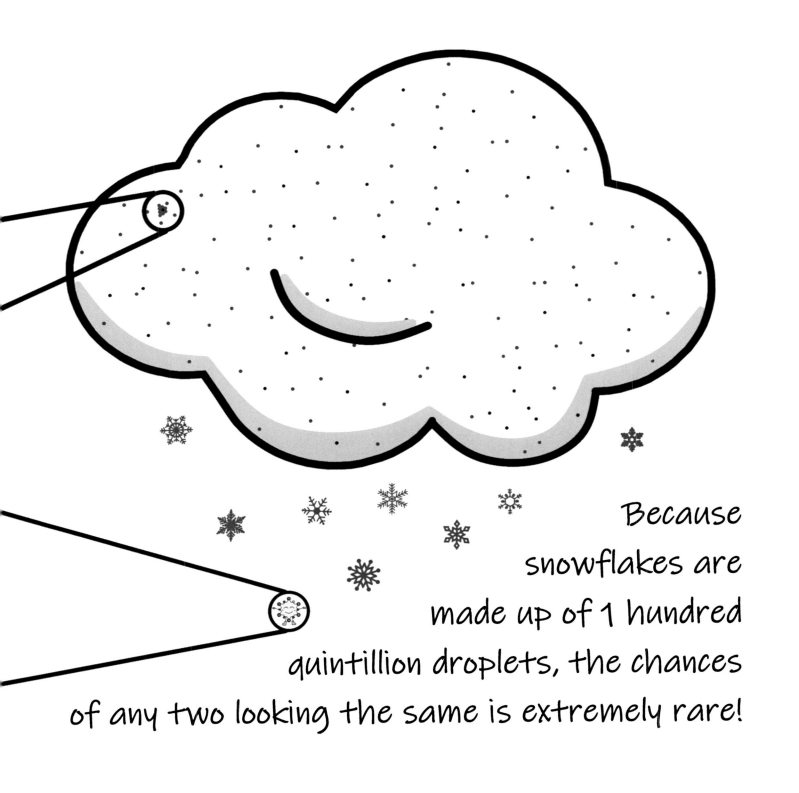

Because snowflakes are made up of 1 hundred quintillion droplets, the chances of any two looking the same is extremely rare!

Sleet starts out like rain, but then travels through a cold patch of air and freezes. This is called a temperature **inversion**.

Hail is formed when warm water droplets are not heavy enough to fall from the cloud yet.

Warm air

A powerful gust of wind pushes them back up into the colder parts of the cloud where they freeze.

This wind is called an

updraft.

Now Harold is heavy enough to fall!

Go, Harold, go!

Today, Harold is going to fall as rain on a mountainside.

When clouds reach a mountain, they are forced to rise, and as they rise, they cool.

Cold air can carry less water than warm air, so the heavy raindrops fall!

When Harold reaches land, he can do a couple of different things.

He can soak into the ground.

This is called **percolation**.

He can be absorbed by plants and then returned to the air when the plant exhales.

This is called **transpiration**.

Groundwater

Or he can run down the mountainside as part of a small stream. This is called

runoff.

Today, Harold decides to go with the flow! Down the mountainside he joins other streams, making a river.

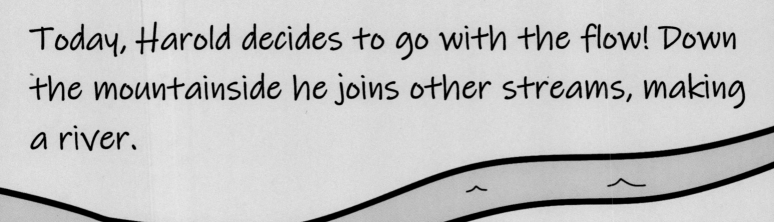

Rivers are an important part of Earth's water cycle. They transport water from high elevations down to low elevations.

There are many different kinds of rivers...

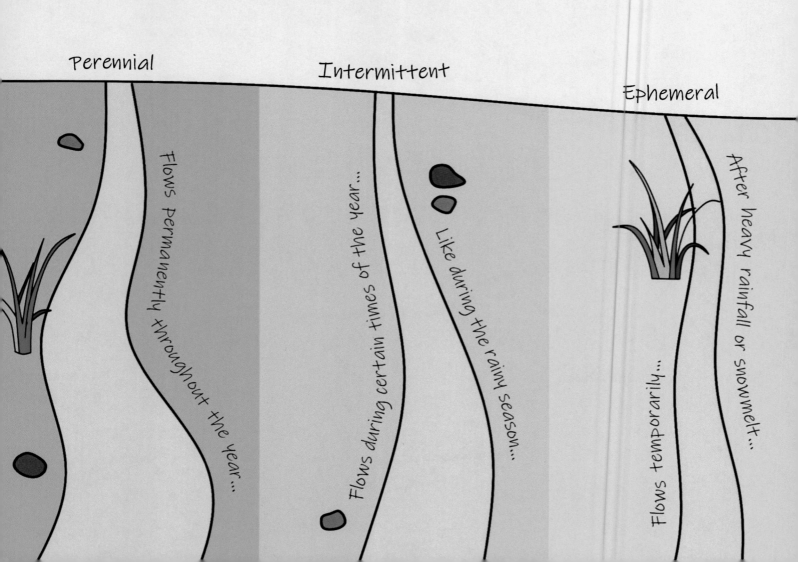

Perennial

Intermittent

Ephemeral

Flows permanently throughout the year...

Flows during certain times of the year...

Like during the rainy season...

Flows temporarily...

After heavy rainfall or snowmelt...

And channels...

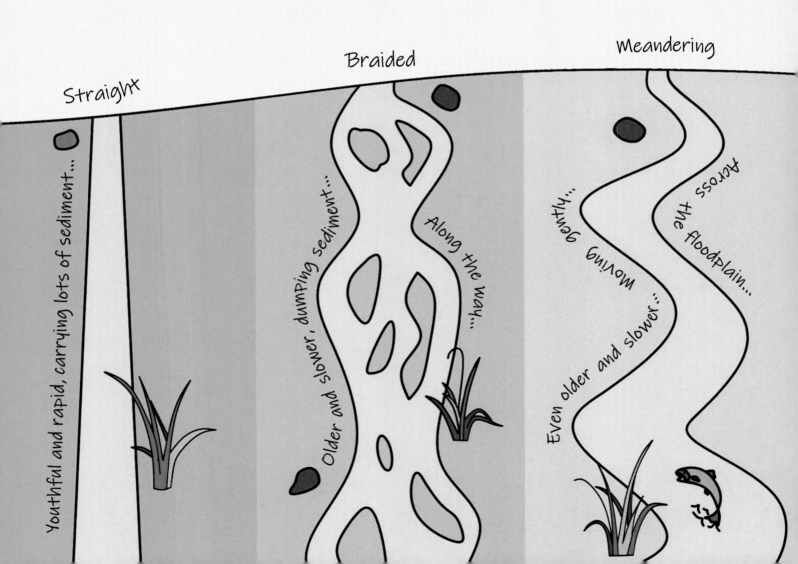

Straight

Braided

Meandering

Youthful and rapid, carrying lots of sediment...

Older and slower, dumping sediment...

Along the way...

Even older and slower...

Moving gently...

Across the floodplain...

Streams and rivers can be **tributaries**.

This means they flow into other rivers or lakes, adding their water to theirs.

Runoff

Runoff

Tributary

Groundwater

Percolation

Together, they form a **watershed**.

Earth has many, many watersheds. Harold's watershed looks like this!

Runoff

Runoff

Tributary

Tributary

Percolation

Lake

Groundwater

Harold has come a long, long way,
and is now in the lake!

Harold now has two choices.
He can stay in the lake or he can go back
into the air...

Harold decides it's time to go home.
To do this, Harold will need to

evaporate.

Evaporation is the process of water moving from a liquid state...

to a gas!

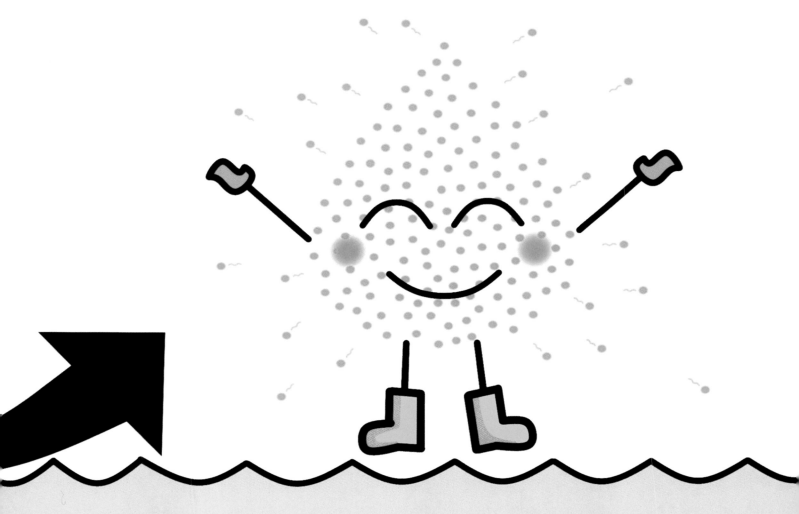

Using the heat from the sun, Harold's water molecules heat up, get lots of energy, and break away from the bonds holding them together. Like they are dancing!

Up, up, up, Harold goes!

His water molecules are losing heat and energy...
Turning back into water droplets. This is called

condensation.

A cloud is formed!

The opposite of evaporation, condensation can happen in one of two ways. Water vapor is either cooled to its dew point or the air becomes so saturated with water vapor, that it can't hold any more water.

Dew point: the temperature at which water vapour in the air condenses to create water droplets.

Harold is now home!

Good job, Harold!

Wow, what a wonderful journey! But how long did it take?

Atmosphere: Water can stay in the atmosphere for approximately 9 days. This is the shortest amount of time water sits in one place as it makes its way through the water system.

Ground: On the Earth's surface, water usually hangs around for a month or two before making its way somewhere else (like a lake).

Groundwater: If water soaks into the ground, and percolates as shallow groundwater, it can stay there for 200 to 300 years. If it moves into deep groundwater systems, it can remain there for 10,000 years.

Snow and glaciers: As a snowflake, water can stay trapped as snowcover for 2 to 6 months, until the spring when it melts. If the water gets trapped in a glacier, it could stay there for 20 to 100 years.

Ocean: If water makes its way to the ocean, it can make its way around the world on different currents. This way, it could stay there for 3,000 years.

Guess I need to get ready for a big long sleep!

Ice shelf: If water makes its way to an ice shelf, such as the arctic, it could get trapped for 900,000 years!

We also learned that matter, like Harold, has three states!

Solid: Solid water has a definite shape and volume. The water particles are closely packed together and have strong intermolecular forces.

Liquid: Liquid water has a definite volume but not a definite shape. The particles are loosely packed and have weak intermolecular forces.

Gas: Water vapour has neither a definite shape nor a definite volume. The particles are far apart and have negligible intermolecular forces.

Thank you so much for learning
about Harold and his water cycle!
See you next time!

Looking for more? Check out some other fantastic reads!

The Bird, The Fish, and The Mouse are Beginner Books for ages 3 to 5. Our friend the Mouse learns tips and tricks to spell new words. The books were inspired by my pet dog, Wylie, who loves to chat with little critters!

There was a Monkey in My Room and *The Christmas Market with Grandma* are Rhyming Books for ages 4 to 6. Rhyming Books teach phonemic awareness, fluency development, and language formation!

Harold the Raindrop and *Sophia the Seed* are Early Reader Books for ages 5 to 7. They are science based, teaching kids about the water and plant life cycles. They were inspired by my children's elementary school teachers!

The Real Life Truth Series is a series of chapter books for ages 8 to 10. They were inspired by my budding story-tellers, Isaac, Philip, and Natalie, who love to tell outlandish stories. When finished, they always claim their stories are "the real-life truth." I hope you live for outlandish tales like they do!

   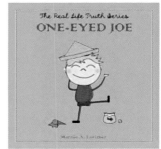

Keep on reading!

Manufactured by Amazon.ca
Bolton, ON

39787646R00026